GOD BLESS THIS
Messy
JOURNAL

GOD BLESS THIS
Messy
JOURNAL

Hannah Brown

HARPER
DESIGN
An Imprint of HarperCollins Publishers

GOD BLESS THIS MESSY JOURNAL

HarperCollins books may be purchased for educational, business, or sales
promotional use. For information, please email the Special Markets Department
at SPsales@harpercollins.com.

First published in 2022 by
Harper Design
An Imprint of HarperCollins*Publishers*
195 Broadway
New York, NY 10007
Tel: (212) 207-7000
Fax: (855) 746-6023
harperdesign@harpercollins.com
hc.com

Distributed throughout the world by
HarperCollinsPublishers
195 Broadway
New York, NY 10007

ISBN 978-0-06-311189-9

Book design by Stislow Design

Photographs/illustrations on page 43 from shutterstock/Kittima05,
pages 72–73, 110–111 from ©shutterstock/keport,
page 85 from ©shutterstock/Baranovskaya,
page 93 from shutterstock/Lili Wave,
page 113 from shutterstock/Liubou Yasiukovich,
page 123 from shutterstock/macondo,
page 132 from shutterstock/JaneHYork

Printed in Malaysia

2nd Printing, 2022

This one is for You. A place where all parts of you are held: your inner child, your deepest fears, your wildest dreams, and the future You who will begin to beam through the pages. I love you already. It's time to love you too.

CONTENTS

hi! ♡

DEAR READER,

Thank you so much for picking up a copy of "God Bless This Messy Journal"! In my recent memoir, "God Bless This Mess," I write about the importance of journaling in my life. So, what better way to experience my love for journaling than to guide you through a personal journaling experience so you can see the magic yourself.

The first time I really committed to journaling was during my junior year of college. I attempted to journal consistently in the past, but my efforts were halfhearted. I tried to bring a notebook with me to church to write sermon notes, but sometimes I would forget to bring the notebook, or I would be too tired.

I can pinpoint the <u>exact</u> day that shifted, because it's recorded on the first page of the first journal I ever finished. It was a Wednesday night during my junior year of college, and I remember that evening vividly because it was my first time getting back to church after struggling with anxiety and depression. I was having a hard time finding the energy to care about my faith, because I was fighting to care about anything. At the time, it was a big step to go to that Wednesday night church sermon; I had just started opening myself up to getting help and trying to figure out what I was going through and how I could feel better. I wrote notes during the sermon, adding my own thoughts and my own prayers to God. I wrote a prayer request list and a couple of words other people said that resonated. I left the sermon feeling, for the first time in a long time, that maybe everything would be okay.

At the beginning, my journaling was exclusively tied to my faith. I committed to writing in my journal after sermons, reflecting on prayers, passages, and conversations from church. Today I still do that, and often write journal entries as prayers. But now I focus much more on how I am feeling, tracking the events of the day to try to understand the emotions that come up. I use my journal to express gratitude and thankfulness for the day-in, day-out life events, for my past, and for the blessing of the future that will come.

Journaling is my outlet where I can write things I don't want to say out loud, and even things that I'm afraid to think. It's a safe space to release negative emotions, and even though it can be scary, I've learned how to be honest with myself and my feelings. Whenever I write, pen to paper, it feels more real. When I first committed to my journaling practice, I was in a bad head space. Writing things down was that first step of real action and taking responsibility for my own mental health and happiness. My goal for journaling has always been the same:

to see real change, to feel real growth.

Journaling is a big, big part of my life now. But no one's perfect. I am definitely not always super motivated to journal. Sometimes I get distracted, sometimes I just don't want to go there, you know? Journaling doesn't really allow you to stay surface level with yourself. I think a lot of people start journaling because they are ready to get honest. And even though being honest and true is sometimes terrifying, it's always worth it. Even when I don't feel like it, I know as soon as I journal, the negative thoughts, the insecurities, the bad energies, and destructive lies will all get much smaller. I'll feel lighter.

I don't think it's possible to journal without getting closer to the source of who you are. Sometimes, it's hard to accept what you find. In the process of journaling, I came up close and personal with hurt— the people who hurt me in the past, the way I've clung to that hurt, and how it showed up in unkind thoughts and toxic habits. It was hard, and it was uncomfortable, but it is what began my process of healing. I discovered the importance of expressed gratitude, the power of manifestation and answered prayers.

Today, I have seven fully completed journals, each page filled with past-Hannah's thoughts, hopes, and struggles. There is nothing quite like reading old entries from the different stages of my life. I wish I could give college-Hannah a hug—tell her to go easier on herself. I've learned so much from "Bachelor"-Hannah—how to be brave and get real. Sometimes, something I've written years ago hits

They're like old friends!

home in the perfect way, almost as if I wrote the words down knowing I would need them later. When I look through my old journals, it's hard not to believe in hope for the future, because I've seen how it has played out so many times before. I've learned that things all really do work together for good. The hurt that feels like it will last forever? It doesn't. Prayers really do get answers (sometimes in mysterious ways), and I'm stronger than I think. Plus, how cool to have years and years of documented change through my journey of life lessons!

This journal is my way of sharing the gift of journaling with you. I'm so excited to show you all the different ways you can use a journal—hint: there is no wrong way! The only mistake you can make while journaling is not being completely truthful with yourself. Like everything else that's worth it, developing a journaling practice isn't easy. It takes time, energy, commitment, and practice. When I journal, my goal is to write about Truth. I want to get to the truth of who I am, who I was made to be. My journals document that journey; now it's time to document yours.

My hope is that you develop your own special relationship with this journal, and that you feel safe in these pages to be vulnerable with yourself. I'm not going to lie to you—this journal isn't the be-all, end-all answer to all of your problems. It's not the thing that is going to change your life overnight. My life is still **messy**. I'm still figuring out how to be happy and how to be the best version of myself. But journaling has transformed the way I approach problems, process emotion, and deal with stress. It is a practice of pure authenticity. It has become a tool to understand, love, and forgive myself. It has taught me how to communicate honestly with others and how to set healthy boundaries. It can be a form of therapy. It allows me to put out in the physical world the heavy thoughts that are holding me back internally. Just like after a therapy session, I always feel better after writing in my journal. That's why we asked two therapists to help with some of the prompts in this book. The first, my very own therapist, Lori Oberacker; and second, Mindy Utay, psychotherapist and licensed certified social worker. Look for their prompts/

exercises throughout the book — I'm so grateful that you'll be able to experience some real therapy yourself!

I like to think of the first half of this journal as a journaling "boot camp." There are prompts and exercises to help you start tapping into who you are and to explore how you're feeling. There are lists,

"THIS IS A SAFE SPACE FOR YOU TO WRITE WHATEVER YOU WANT WITH ZERO JUDGMENT."

activities, and prompts from a real therapist for you to answer, and even examples from my own journal entries to guide different types of reflection. In the second half of the journal, the training wheels come off. This is where you can really make this journal your own and take that leap of faith. I've included some of my favorite lyrics, quotes, and Bible verses to inspire your writing, but I challenge you to develop your own relationship with these pages.

This is a safe space for you to write whatever you want with zero judgment. The world can be so critical, and everyone sees things from different perspectives. Embrace this space of freedom and don't worry about "saying the right thing." I want this journal to be your therapeutic best friend and a place of daily solace. Find the courage to be vulnerable, be honest with yourself, and don't be afraid to get messy!

Love, ♡
Hannah

XOXO

PART 1

Let's do this together! →

1.

Who Am I?

"I *am* enough. I am loved. No more, no less. That's all that matters. And to really believe that—well, that's the goal. Some days I do. Other days, I'm not quite there yet. And that's okay. Because I know it's the journey I'm on now. I know I'll get there."

—HANNAH BROWN, *GOD BLESS THIS MESS*

WHAT MAKES YOU, YOU?

The more I journal and get to know myself, the more I realize how much my childhood impacted me. Reflecting on the things, places, and people that made me happy when I was younger helps me reflect on my current happiness. Have I lost track of the things I'm passionate about, the things that gave me the most joy? So, before we get to who you are now, describe who you *were*.

Five adjectives to describe yourself as a child:

1. Shy
2. Sister
3. Tomboy
4. ~~scared~~ Afraid of getting in trouble
5. Foodie

What were you favorite subjects in school?

Pe, art, year book

Who were the most influential teachers you had in school?

Stone, RO, ?

What were your favorite sports or hobbies when you were younger?

To Play outside, soccer, Gym

What were your favorite books growing up?

movies? :)

What were the first things you did that made you feel confident?

soccer, track, RUNNing

Isn't it nice to see all these things on one page?

WHO YOU ARE

Now let's dig a little deeper into who you really are today, in this moment. Don't think too hard or judge yourself for what you write down—as long as your answers feel true to you, they're right!

Five adjectives you use to describe yourself now:

These are mine.

1. Authentic
2. Honest
3. Resilient
4. Self-aware
5. Brave

Five adjectives you use to describe yourself now:

1. Realistic
2. Honest
3. Upfront
4. Self aware
5. Guilty

Who are your mentors—people you look up to and who influence how you want your life and career to look like?

Jesus, Sister, Tonya

What things are you really passionate about and feel you excel at?

Gym, friends, cooking/learning to

Describe where you live now.

w/ Letilea (renting)

Describe your professional life, or, if you're in school, your education.

Skyscene

Do you have any side hustles? If you had a side hustle and could turn it into your full-time job, what would it be?

No But I should think about it.

CHECKING IN

My therapist, Lori Oberacker MS, LMHC, Professional/Personal Life Coach, has been a major part of my journaling practice. She keeps me on track and gives me incredible prompts for self-reflection. You'll see more prompts from Lori throughout this journal that she's given ~~me~~ US—I'm excited to share them! So what better way to start than with this super-simple check-in exercise. Answer the following questions as honestly as you can.

What am I **hogging** in my life (things that are taking up the most headspace)?

Netfred, Shows, How to edd things w/ barrette

What am I **frogging** in my life (skipping to other topics or avoiding)?

What am I **flogging** in my life (beating a topic to death)?

FAVORITES

What do you like to do the most? What makes you happy? Answer the questions below, and feel free to expand on why! I've included some of my favorites too.

What are your favorite hobbies or physical activities?

Riding my bike, long walks, yoga, dancing, paddleboarding

What are your favorite ways to exercise?

Dancing, yoga, boxing

What are your favorite foods?

Homemade cookies, berries, breakfast burritos, a good cheeseburger, Mediterranean food, avocados, a vibrant salad

What is your favorite book?

"Redeeming Love" by Francine Rivers

What are your favorite movies?

My favorite "easy-watching" movies are "Hope Floats," "Sweet Home Alabama," "The Notebook," and "Bridesmaids." I also love Disney animated movies—escapism at its finest. "Life of Pi" is also one of my favorites.

What are your favorite TV shows?

Here's a fun fact about me:
I hate watching TV series that have more than
3-4 seasons max, but that's really pushing it.
I love "Bridgerton," "The Wilds," "Big Little Lies,"
and "New Girl"!

What are your favorite flowers?

I've always had a special thing with tulips. My
godmother, who was my first babysitter, was the
first bride I had ever seen. I was the flower
girl and I remember going with her for her bridal
portraits. We went to this garden of tulips. Seeing
her in her beautiful wedding gown, smiling while
surrounded by tulips, I think associated the tulips
with love. I also love an English rose, peonies,
ranunculus, and hydrangeas. I'm a big flower girl
and love to keep fresh flowers in my house!

What are your favorite scents?

Lavender, cinnamon, bark/cedar smell, palo santo,
musk, magnolia, Fraser fir, eucalyptus

FAVORITES

What are your favorite hobbies or physical activities?

_____

_____

_____

What are your favorite ways to exercise?

_____

_____

_____

What are your favorite foods?

_____

_____

_____

What is your favorite book?

_____

_____

_____

What are your favorite movies?

_____

_____

_____

What are your favorite TV shows?

_____

_____

_____

What are your favorite flowers?

_____

_____

_____

What are your favorite scents?

_____

_____

_____

Yes! I just love scents.
They can really change
the whole atmosphere
of a space.

LIST OF WORDS OR PHRASES

Making a list is an easy way to get down thoughts spontaneously, and I think a great first step in getting comfortable with your journal. Write a list of words or phrases that describe who you are, what you're looking for, and where you are. Don't overthink—whatever words or phrases come to mind, write them down!

Here is an example of one I wrote:

- Strong
- Vulnerable
- Fearless—no fear
- Don't forget who I am, but continue learning who I am—and embracing that
- Worthy
- Goofy
- Messy
- Beautiful
- Looking for freedom
- Becoming empowered

- Open and ready for life
- Honest
- Accepting
- Open to new adventures
- Brave
- Growing
- Trying to find truth/ stay true
- On a journey
- Unconditional love
- Fear that knows no bounds
- Looking for understanding

LIST OF WORDS OR PHRASES

Now, your turn.

When I'm having a sad day, this is one of my go-to ways to turn my day around. I write a list of everything I can think of that I love. Something about naming the **people**, **foods**, **feelings**, **activities—really anything and everything that brings me joy**—reminds me that I have so much to be grateful for. It can also serve as a big brainstorm of ways to pull myself out of a funk. So, practice writing a list of anything that makes you feel good. Here's a list from my journal:

- Morning coffee 🕐 (until noon)
- Brunch
- Snuggles
- The way babies smell
- Lavender
- Fresh flowers
- Nutter Butters
- Baked goods 🥖
- That feeling after a workout (a good one)
- Deep conversations
- Meeting friendly strangers
- The way music can do incredible things
- Creating a good outfit
- The way fabric (expensive, good quality) feels
- Sunny and 75 degrees
- Feeling confident
- Greenery 🌿
- Trees
- White houses
- A well-designed room
- Puppies
- Disney!
- Island/beach life ⛱
- Feeling pretty without makeup—clear skin
- Tan skin
- Bare skin
- A good kiss
- Funny people
- Fruit
- How words can heal, give clarity
- A well-lit room 💡
- A good idea
- The perfect buzz
- Dancing (giving no effs)
- The way a man looks at you (googly eyes)
- Clean sheets out of the dryer
- The Holy Spirit's presence

THINGS I LOVE

2.

WHAT DO I WANT to BE?

"Trust the wait. Embrace the uncertainty.
Enjoy the beauty of becoming. When nothing
is certain, anything is possible."

—MANDY HALE

ADJECTIVES THAT DESCRIBE
WHAT I WANT TO BE

It's a big question, which is why I think a creative list is the perfect way to approach it. Don't overthink, just write down adjectives that you associate with the best version of yourself, and what you want to be. Here's an example of a list I made:

- Brave
- Courageous
- Joyful
- Empathetic
- Strong
- Beautiful
- A leader
- Patient
- Resilient
- Accepting
- Present
- Hopeful
- Grateful
- Gracious
- Content

- Determined
- Motivated
- Inspired
- Creative
- Humble
- Vulnerable
- Smart
- Kind
- Assertive
- Genuine
- Faithful
- Free
- Loving/loved
- Encouraging
- Independent

- Dependable
- Forgiving
- Self-compassionate
- Adventurous
- Responsible
- Silly
- Enough.
  And no more.
  No less.
  Believe it ♥

WHAT DO I WANT TO BE?

ROUTINE

Thinking about who you want to be is complicated, but a good place to start is by writing down clear goals and intentions. Goals can be overwhelming and intimidating, so try thinking about how you want to structure your day—how you can create a routine that will help you become the best version of yourself. Here are some questions about routine to get you started. Every day is different, but here's an example of my morning and evening routine.

What is your morning routine?

My morning routine starts with me sleepy-eyed, walking to the kitchen. I try to be good and drink water with lemon first thing . . . but sometimes the coffee can't wait! I drink a hot black coffee as I cuddle up in my favorite blanket on the couch. Being productive first thing is hard for me. I actually love mornings, but I have sleep conditions that make it a little harder for me to wake up in the morning. I like to enjoy my mornings, and I enjoy my morning routine. I change up the order sometimes, but I sit and read for a little, journal, read my devotion, my Bible, pray, and meditate. I also try to stretch a little. I make up my bed and tidy up the living space.

What is your bedtime routine?

I have gotten into the habit of really trying to make my bedroom a sacred space for rest. So sometimes I think my body knows it's time to go to bed as soon as I go into my room. I make sure in the evenings to keep a dim lamp on in my room, and often a candle burning. I love a calming tea right before bed too. I also really like to read a few pages of a "light" book before I go to bed. Sometimes, if for some reason I'm still really wound up from the day's events, it's a show like "New Girl" or a Disney movie for a few minutes. I just try to spend a little bit calming down so I can ease into sleepy time!

good morning!

make it
happen

nighty-night

What is your morning routine?

_____

_____

_____

_____

_____

What is your bedtime routine?

_____

_____

_____

_____

_____

What do you want your morning routine to look like?

_____

_____

_____

_____

What do you want your bedtime routine to look like?

_____

_____

_____

_____

_____

What is one thing that you commit to changing about your current morning routine that will make it look more like what you want it to look like?

_____

_____

_____

_____

_____

What is one thing that you commit to changing about your current bedtime routine that will make it look more like what you want it to look like?

_____

_____

_____

_____

_____

"God, you have so much planned for me. I want to grow into the person you designed me to be. Expose some of these unused gifts you have instilled in me. I will put myself out there to be a vessel. No fear."

INTENTIONS AND POTENTIALS

If you could wave a magic wand, what would each day look like? How would you feel? What do you want for yourself professionally, romantically, for your health? Writing down intentions and potentials in your journal is a good exercise to check in with your growth, see if you're on track for your goals, and help figure out what's working for you and what is no longer serving you. This kind of reflection is what I find spurs the most personal growth—manifestation is powerful, and articulating your goals consistently forces you to hold yourself accountable.

Something I often need!

What are some "potentials" of mine? Potentials can be unused abilities, reserved strengths, unused success, dormant gifts, hidden talents, and more.

BUCKET LIST

I love bucket lists. They remind me to dream BIG, and they help me write down things I want to do that I don't usually make time for. It's a mix of dreams that are crazy and adventurous, and dreams that are free and attainable—something I've seen in a movie that I've always wanted to try, or a new hobby that might turn into a passion. Silly or serious, a bucket list should be a massive jumble of things that might make you happy. Here's one that I wrote awhile back, before I was on *The Bachelor*:

- Dance in the rain
- Go on an African safari
- See the Grand Canyon
- See the Northern Lights
- Watch a meteor shower
- Write something? Blog, book?
- Spend a long summer on the beach
- Stargaze in back of a pickup truck
- Go to Greece!
- Be in a music video (country, duh!)
- See the Seven Wonders of the World
- Visit the glow-worm cave in New Zealand
- Spin clay thing— make pottery
- Take martial arts class
- Learn ballroom dancing
- Paris! Eat macarons and see the Eiffel Tower
- Fly first class
- Be a foster home/family if it's the Lord's will
- Change someone's life financially, give a huge gift to
- Be on Ellen* ——▷

BUCKET LIST

*When I wrote "be on Ellen," I meant sitting in the audience.
Never did I think I would be a guest that Ellen interviewed
a few years later!

3.

How Do I Get There?

"The one who falls and gets up is so much
stronger than the one who never fell."

—ROY T. BENNETT

A CREATIVE MEETING
WITH MYSELF

"Getting there" is a process. I like to think about identifying what I want my
future to look like and my goals as having creative meetings with myself.
I write down every idea, big or small, with no judgment. No ideas are bad
or wrong, too small or too big—anything that makes me feel excited and
motivated works. I wrote this list after I went home from *The Bachelor* and was
feeling super lost. I didn't know what I was going to do. I was broke, had just
been on this TV show, and had no idea what was going to happen next. So,
I made a list of words that represented everything I wanted to be aligned with
in whatever career I created:

- Be a face; host
- Honesty
- Beauty
- Feels good/feels right
- Fun
- Comforting
- Relationships
- Familiarity
- Communication
- Individuality
- Unique
- Music

- Interesting people
- Sharing stories
- Laughter
- Strong
- JESUS
- Southern
- Country
- Authenticity
- Admitting failures
- Wisdom winks and wake-ups
- Engagements

- A financially stable life; live comfortably
- Have a qualified team to help
- Gain access to events/celebs
- Do promotions
- Collaborate with other brands/people in the industry
- Trial and error of new things
- Adventures/bucket list items/travel/see the world and see it differently
- See how others live
- Be able to really help people with what I've been given
- Country music baby!
- Dancing with the stars!
- Spokesperson for brands that align with ideals.

A CREATIVE MEETING WITH MYSELF

Reflect on your creative meeting. What goals do you need to set to work toward the things you identified in your creative meeting that represent **who** you want to be and **what** you want to be aligned with?

Try writing down five goals for each of the categories. I know that naming goals can be scary and stressful, but remember: these are just for **you**. You're going to look back at this list and realize that your goals then are different from your goals now. Use this list as a checkpoint for later, to help you stay aligned. If something bumps you off your path or you feel left of center, it might be because you've changed, and these goals no longer suit you. This journal is your safe space—it's okay to write it down, and it doesn't have to come true! Try to use this as an exercise for manifestation and self-reflection.

FIVE CAREER GOALS:

1. _____

2. _____

3. _____

4. _____

5. _____

FIVE DATING/RELATIONSHIP GOALS:

1. _____

2. _____

3. _____

4. _____

5. _____

FIVE SELF-LOVE AND SELF-CARE GOALS:

1. _____

2. _____

3. _____

4. _____

5. _____

LISTS OF FIVE—PLANNING

Now that you've identified a bunch of goals for your career, relationships, and self-care, pick one goal from each. You can pick the easiest one to reach, the one that's most important to you, or even the one that might be the most difficult to accomplish. What you choose to expand on is totally up to you. Ask yourself:

How will you make these goals a reality?
What concrete steps will you take to make these goals happen?
How long will you give yourself to make them a reality?

PLAN FOR ONE CAREER GOAL:

_____

_____

_____

_____

_____

_____

_____

_____

_____

_____

_____

_____

PLAN FOR ONE DATING/RELATIONSHIP GOAL:

PLAN FOR ONE SELF-LOVE AND SELF-CARE GOAL:

"If you are one of those people who has that little voice in the back of her mind saying, 'Maybe I could do [fill in the blank],' DON'T tell it to be quiet. Give it a little room to grow, and try to find an environment it can grow in."

-Reese Witherspoon

AFFIRMATIONS & MANTRAS

For this exercise, I asked my therapist, Lori, to weigh in on what exactly affirmations are and how we can use them. I really like the way she explained it to me, so I wanted to share with you!

This is what she said:

Affirmations and **personal mantras** are statements you say to yourself in a repetitive way. Affirmations have been used in psychology for years as part of the healing process for clients, with different degrees of success. Mantras have been used for thousands of years by monks to train their mind. Both affirmations and mantras are methods of focused attention and concentration. We use them to change different aspects of our lives. A person's success is based on the number of repetitions and their level of commitment to positive growth.

LOVE

I begin and end my day by **loving**
and **accepting** who I am

I am **loving** and **lovable**

I **know** my forever partner is out there

I love and honor my **inner child**

HEALTH

I make time to simply be **me**

I am **always** taken care of

I am **whole** and I am **healthy**

I thank God for this **beautiful temple**
he made in me

CAREER

Today is the perfect day to imagine and
create a better future for me

I am **confident** and **calm**

I can **handle** any obstacles in my path

I have **huge potential** and **believe** in myself

Getting in the practice of writing affirmations is a great way to stay positive and focused on your goals. For me, affirmations were uncomfortable at first. I struggled with my confidence, so it felt weird to write down something so overwhelmingly positive about myself or an aspect of my life. Sometimes I read the affirmations I write out loud. It can be scary, but it's had a big impact on my self-confidence.

Start by writing an affirmation for one of the goals in each category below.

CAREER GOAL:

_____

_____

_____

AFFIRMATION:

_____

_____

_____

_____

LOVE GOAL:

_____

_____

_____

AFFIRMATION:

_____

_____

_____

_____

HEALTH GOAL:

_____

_____

_____

AFFIRMATION:

_____

_____

_____

_____

Imagine this: → One year from today, you've been working your hardest toward all the goals you listed above. You made the changes, you did your best to **stick to the plan**. Describe what your life looks like after a year of doing the work. What is your job like, your relationships, your mental health, your physical health? Try to be specific about how that future self feels and acts.

Sounds pretty good, right? Sometimes it's
hard to stay motivated and keep the
momentum going. A lot of bigger goals aren't
reachable in a day. But I like to visualize
what the absolute best version of myself
might look like. The clearer I can see her,
the more determined I am to become her.

REFLECTION

When you set a goal, what tends to stop you from attaining it?
What roadblocks do you encounter and how do you typically respond?*

_____

_____

_____

_____

_____

_____

_____

_____

_____

_____

_____

_____

_____

_____

*This is a question from Mindy Utay, psychotherapist and
licensed certified social worker. You'll see a few more questions
from her throughout the journal!

PERSONAL MANTRA

The word **mantra** comes from *manas* (mind) and *tra* (liberation, truth, tool), so I guess many things could be mantras from this explanation, but generally a mantra may be considered a phrase, word, or prayer that we repeat either silently or aloud.

This is another great exercise that my therapist, Lori, asked me to do! Crafting a personal mantra is a powerful tool in my self-care toolkit. I've created mantras for lots of different reasons—for when I'm feeling insecure, for when I'm feeling overwhelmed, for when I feel like I need to relax—and even though it might seem silly to repeat a phrase over and over, believe me when I tell you they can be super effective.

How to Create a Mantra
Make a list of three things that you want to change in your life.
Use the phrase "I am." For example, "I am anxious" or "I am stuck."

1. _____

2. _____

3. _____

For each of these three things, write down the opposite phrase.
"I am at peace" and "I am moving forward."

1. _____

2. _____

3. _____

Now string these positive revelations together in an affirmative statement in an order that feels good to you. For example, "I am at peace and purposely moving forward today with a positive attitude."

1. _____

2. _____

3. _____

Type or handwrite your phrase on an index card or note card. Place it somewhere you will see it throughout your day. You can tape it to your bathroom mirror, car, computer screen, or refrigerator door. Repeat it to yourself several times throughout the day, silently or aloud. Make it a habit—first thing in the morning, before you go to bed, and anytime you find yourself focusing on the very things your mantra is intended to change.

Keep this mantra for as long as it feels helpful. At any time you can go through these steps and create a new mantra to change other aspects of your life. Your mantra needs commitment and practice to really work. It may not work overnight, but if you work on practicing it and allow your mantra to get into your bones, over time you will find that it helps you become calmer and more centered.

Say it. Repeat it. Share it. Live it.

If any positive quotes or sayings resonate deeply with you, they can be personal mantras too.

MINI COLLAGE

Use these two pages to create a collage in your journal! Cut and paste images that speak to your soul. Use old photos, images, patterns, backgrounds, words and/or phrases to create something that symbolizes you.

This is just a little taste
of what you can do — you
can create a bigger version
on a poster board.
I love collaging my emotions,
feelings, and dreams.

4.

Getting Messy!

"My life really was a complete mess, and God bless all of it. Because it's in the messes where we learn the most—as long as we slow down enough to realize what God is trying to show us."

—HANNAH BROWN, *GOD BLESS THIS MESS*

Now it's time to get real. Consider the previous three parts of the journal your warm-up. It's time to dig deep and practice honesty. One of the hardest parts about journaling is forcing yourself to be 100 percent honest with yourself about your most vulnerable moments. It definitely takes courage, but I am here to help you take that leap.

HOW I FEEL

When I'm struggling, sometimes I try to identify how I feel. Naming these feelings helps me get to the *why*—I start identifying patterns. Try writing a list of how you felt the last time you were hitting a low. Here is an example of a list I wrote around the same time I wrote the list of future goals. Right after I was on *The Bachelor*, but before *The Bachelorette*, I was having a tough time. I didn't have a plan and I was working toward coming to terms with everything that happened on *The Bachelor*. So I wrote a list of all the negative emotions that were starting to overwhelm me. It was emotional, but I felt so much better having put a name to these feelings. Once I named them, they weren't as intimidating:

- Lonely
- No one around me understands
- Lazy
- No motivation
- No direction
- Waiting game
- Hopeful
- Restless
- Embarrassed
- Confused

- Discontent
- Jealous of other peoples' relationships/life advancing

HOW I FEEL

HOW TO FEEL BETTER

After I wrote the list about how I felt, I wrote a list about what I could do to feel better. I focused on the smaller things that I could control. Sometimes when you're feeling low, a task as simple as cleaning your room or going for a walk is the solution. You don't have to tackle all your problems in one day. Really little things are often the most helpful at pulling you out of a funk. Here's my list of things to do to feel better:

Mine

- Eat better
- Get exercise (start daily) → get up early!
- Don't look at the phone as much
- Talk to friends who do/don't understand bad stuff
- Talk to Mom about job starting ASAP
- Clean out and clear out my living space (get clothes/closet/life in order)
- Make time to be with friends because you have the time
- Keep journaling/reflecting/filling up good stuff
- Pray! Put burdens on Jesus.

Yours

Mindy gave me this question — it
helps me think critically about how
I choose to self-soothe.

When you are tense or anxious, what are your coping skills for dealing with those feelings?

_____

_____

_____

_____

_____

_____

_____

_____

_____

_____

_____

_____

_____

_____

_____

_____

_____

MY STRUGGLES

Identifying your struggles is an important step in being honest with yourself. Even if there's a part of you that you're scared to face, the longer you avoid the things that are hurting you, the longer those struggles will hold you back. List the things that you struggle with. Here is an example from my own journal:

- I don't feel good enough
- I think my recognition = my happiness and my value
- I feel like I have to prove my worth
- I strive, strive, strive
- I discourage myself with negative self-talk
- I am not motivated to do anything
- I struggle to be kind to myself
- I get overwhelmed and retreat and isolate from everyone

MY STRUGGLES

This is hard, but you can do it!

If you made it
down here, nice job.

COLOR INSIDE A HEART

Fun! → Fill in different parts of this heart with emotions you're feeling **right now**. Feel free to use different words/phrases, drawings/doodles, or different colors to represent your heart.

*You might call this art therapy, but I call it heart therapy! Thanks, Lori, for this beautiful exercise!

WRITE A POEM

Writing a poem is a great way to flex your creative muscles and try to articulate emotions or process events. Try to let go of any judgment of whether the poem is "good" or "bad"—no one has to see or read this unless you choose to share!

Here's an example of a poem I wrote.

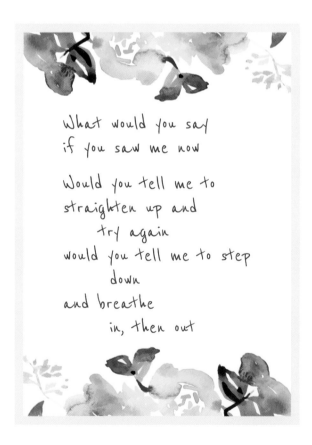

What would you say
if you saw me now

Would you tell me to
straighten up and
      try again
would you tell me to step
      down
and breathe
      in, then out

WRITE A POEM

YOUR MESSIEST MOMENTS

Sometimes life gets messy. Here are some prompts to help reflect on those times. I encourage you to get down as much detail as possible and really be honest with yourself. Try to avoid assigning blame and, as always, be gentle and kind to yourself. **Bless these messy moments!**

What was one of the biggest conflicts you've been in? Describe who it was with, how it started, and the resolution (if it was resolved).

What are your biggest regrets?

What were your most embarrassing moments?

Remember, no one is going
to see this but you.

_____

_____

_____

_____

_____

_____

_____

_____

_____

_____

_____

_____

_____

_____

_____

_____

_____

_____

_____

_____

_____

Describe a time in your life when you felt really low. What were you struggling with? How did you recover?

YOUR HAPPIEST MOMENTS

Reflecting on the times that you have been happy is just as important as reflecting on your messiest moments. Here are some prompts to help reflect on the best of times.

Describe a time in your life you were really proud of yourself.

_____

_____

_____

_____

_____

_____

_____

_____

_____

_____

_____

_____

_____

Describe one of your favorite days last year. What were you doing? Who were you with?

_____

_____

_____

_____

_____

_____

_____

_____

_____

_____

_____

_____

_____

_____

_____

_____

_____

_____

_____

Best day ever!!!

O.K.! I've had my fair share of drama when it comes to romantic relationships—a lot of that drama unfolded in front of millions of people. Sometimes the **criticism**, **hate**, and **judgment** were overwhelming. My journal was my safe place where I could process what was happening, figure out _not always easy_ how I was feeling, and block out all that extra noise. Here are some prompts that I find helpful when I'm trying to reflect on romantic relationships.

If you've never been in a romantic relationship, if you have in the past but aren't currently, or if you are in one now, I think it's still helpful to think about what you want and why you want it.

WHAT DO I WANT FROM A PARTNER?

Make a list of all the things you want from a romantic partner. These could be things you want from a partner you haven't met yet, or maybe things you want with your current partner. Here's an example from a journal entry from 2017—this is definitely personal to me, and what I wanted then is different from what I want now, but it's a good example of the exercise:

- Love, serve, lead me
- I try to think back on my relationships because I think I learned a lot about what I do/don't want from my past experiences and am so thankful for the heartbreak, for what I've been through
- I want FUN → to be loved and to love should be fun! Someone who will make me laugh and be goofy with me and love that I'm a weirdo
- Hard worker—can't stop, won't stop.

- A good family. Family is important to him.
- Great with kids, children are drawn to him.
- Someone who challenges me. Calls me on my crap.
- Passionate love that's undeniable
- He is who he is, unapologetically
- Intelligent
- Religious → loves Jesus
- Respectable → others respect him because he respects others

WHAT DO I WANT FROM A PARTNER?

What do you REALLY want???
↘

The questions on the next four pages are all from Lori.
They've really helped me think about my relationships.

When you think about the person you want to be with, or the person you are with, what are your feelings? What makes you feel safe in the relationship? What memories are attached to those feelings?

_____

_____

_____

_____

_____

_____

_____

_____

In a romantic relationship, what are the qualities of great communication?

_____

_____

_____

_____

_____

_____

_____

_____

_____

How do you show love in a romantic relationship? What do others do to make you feel loved?

Write a prayer for a romantic partner—whether or not you've met that person or they are already in your life, write about how you want to bless them and what you wish for them.

I loved thinking about the ways I wanted to bless my partner. ♡

Here's an example of a list of prayers I wrote:

- Protection. Cover him. Remove any temptation or evil from his path, Father. Help him be quick to respond and know when the enemy is attacking and that he would have strength to prevail.
- Wash over him with a mighty wave of peace.
- Have favor over him, but also place on his heart the desire to serve and honor you with every action and word.
- I pray he loves you with all his heart, soul, mind, and strength.
- I pray he can clearly communicate with others, and me, and use his words to comfort and encourage me in times of need.

THE THINGS I LOVE ABOUT
MY PARTNER

Write a list of all the things you love about your romantic partner. If you don't have a partner, write a list of all the things you *want* to love in a future partner. Here is a list I wrote—some of it's silly and simple, but as a whole I love how it reflects the relationship I'm in now and have always wanted to have.

- His confidence
- His ability to be present
- His eyes
- His perfect teeth
- His level-headedness
- His "swagger"
- How he listens to me
- How he looks at me
- He always cleans up and helps me
- He helps me slow down
- He encourages me

- He tells me how beautiful I am (even when I don't understand)
- I feel admired and adored
- His snuggles
- How he feels safe
- How his hand fits with mine holding hands
- He helps me look cooler
- He makes me feel like I should be confident
- He's a rock—and loves my star shine
- How he smells

- He's sophisticated, and manly, and artsy, and a smoke show all at the same time
- How he loves his family/ comes from a sweet family
- **He makes me feel special**
- We are different, not competitive—more uplifting
- How he lets me process how I feel, and adds understanding
- How he leads and encourages me to do the right thing
- How he believes in and supports my dreams
- How sure he is that we will make all the things we manifest come true
- How he brings me "happys"

- How he loves sunsets and being outside
- How we take sweet afternoon naps
- How we both create together
- **How he steps up when I need a little extra help**
- How he really is my #1 fan
- **How he loves when I just lay on him**
- How he always dances with me
- His love notes ♡
- **He juggles! I love it.**
- Our midday Facetimes

FAMILY AND SUPPORT

Family can be so many things. It can be who you're related to, who you lean on most for support, your best friends, your mentors, your colleagues. Family looks and feels different to everyone. I love thinking about my biological and my created families as one big unit of support. Sometimes when I'm feeling down, I like to list the people in my family. It's a good reminder that you're not as alone as you feel, and a way to honor the people around you.

List the people that you consider family.

_____

_____

_____

_____

_____

_____

_____

_____

_____

_____

_____

_____

_____

_____

Lori pushes me to expand my definition of family —
I love this exercise from her!

Often, the people who support you and that you consider family are connected
in direct or indirect ways. Draw a family tree of support—think about the
surprising ways some of these people are connected.

REFLECTING ON FAMILY

Mindy believes that examining your family dynamics and childhood is an important part of understanding yourself. The questions on the next 4 pages are all from her!

How did your family talk about emotions when you were growing up, if at all?

_____

_____

_____

_____

_____

_____

_____

_____

_____

_____

_____

_____

_____

_____

_____

_____

Who did you go to if you had a problem as a child? Why?

What were the strengths in your family? The weaknesses?

What is your earliest memory of feeling connected in your family?
Of feeling isolated or alone?

REFLECTING ON FRIENDSHIP

I've always believed in a handful of friends versus a ~~bunch of acquaintances~~ X who just fill space. I've had to learn that the people who love me, love me the way I am. The people in my life don't want anything from me other than shared, meaningful, life-giving time together. Even though I don't see my friends from back home, whenever we get back together, it's like nothing has changed. That's the kind of friendship I look for now. Friends who are understanding when I fall, don't put pressure on me . . . and know to voice memo or call because I am a terrible texter.

A good friend looks different to everyone, because everyone needs different kinds of support and lives a different lifestyle. Maybe you need a friend who is a good listener, or maybe you need a friend who is good at giving you space. What do you need in a good friend? List five words or phrases that describe what you want in a friend.

1.

2.

3.

4.

5.

Quality friendships over quantity!

Do you think you're a good friend? Reflect on times you were a good friend and times you wish you were a better friend.

GRATITUDE

I've gotten in the practice of writing gratitude lists. It helps remind me of all the things in my life I take for granted and helps me stay optimistic. I try to write at least ten every day as a running list—it's so satisfying to see the hundreds of things I'm grateful for.

5/15/2021

31. I am grateful for Adam's support
32. I am grateful for healing
33. I am grateful for wealth to cover my health and fitness journey
34. I am grateful for coffee
35. I am grateful for birthday parties
36. I am grateful for Sully
37. I am grateful for puppies
38. I am grateful for good sleep
39. I am grateful for new shoes
40. I am thankful for a warm bed to sleep in

5/23/2021

81. I am grateful for red wagon rides
82. I am grateful for the wind
83. I am grateful for comfy green grass

84. I am grateful for viby music
85. I am grateful for pretty weather days
86. I am grateful for my car
87. I am grateful for a nice place to live
88. I am grateful for relaxing days
89. I am grateful to live by the ocean
90. I am grateful for live music
91. I am grateful for PINK
92. I am grateful for cute clothes

6/8/2021
136. I am grateful for constructive conversation
137. I am grateful for Adam
138. I am grateful for breath
139. I am grateful for yoga
140. I am grateful for Scripture
141. I am grateful for connection
142. I am grateful for working out
143. I am grateful for podcasts to learn from
144. I am grateful for therapy
145. I am grateful for experience

★ CHALLENGE: try to implement writing ten things every day—
see how you feel doing this for a week!

GRATITUDE LIST

Practice by writing ten things you're grateful for today—from your morning coffee to a phone call with a friend, they can be little things or big things:

_____

_____

_____

_____

_____

_____

_____

_____

GRATITUDE

Visually document the things you are grateful for: what do these things, people, feelings, places, etc. look like? Use the space below to draw.

THANK YOU!

 On my list every day!

GRATITUDE LETTERS

Write a letter to the person you are most grateful for. What do you want to tell them? How do you want to thank them?

LETTER TO YOUR FUTURE SELF

I love reading my old journals. They remind me of how far I've come and often inspire me to keep pushing forward. In a way, each time I journal, I'm writing a letter to my future self. Use this space to write a letter to yourself to read in **five years**. What do you want future-you to know? What predictions do you have? Who and where do you hope to be?

Date five years from today: _____

Hi!

_____

_____

_____

_____

_____

_____

_____

_____

_____

_____

_____

_____

_____

_____

_____

_____

_____

_____

_____

LETTER TO YOUR PAST SELF

What is something you wish you could tell your past self? Think of a time in your life when you could have used some help, and write a letter to that version of yourself.

_____

_____

_____

_____

_____

_____

_____

_____

_____

_____

_____

_____

_____

_____

_____

_____

_____

129

PROMPTS FOR REFLECTING
ON GROWTH

Lori has taught me how important it is to examine the different parts of past, present, and future me. The next four pages are prompts from her that have helped me grow.

↘ How have you changed in the past year? In the past five years?

_____

_____

_____

_____

_____

_____

_____

_____

_____

_____

_____

_____

_____

_____

_____

_____

What do you need more of in life? Less of?

CALMING COLORS

Create a drawing or painting on this page using colors that calm you.

Feel free to use any medium!
Personally, I love watercolor. ♡

FAVORITE QUOTE OR SCRIPTURE

Draw your favorite quote or Scripture verse. Take words of wisdom from somewhere else—maybe the lyrics to your favorite song or your favorite prayer—and turn them into something visually inspiring. Re-create the words in a creative and completely unique way.

"

"

YOUR SECRETS

Everyone has secrets. Trust your journal as a space where you can share them. Use the space below to write the things you've never told anyone—something that happened, something you did, a way you feel, a thing you saw.

QUESTIONS FROM A REAL THERAPIST | THERAPY SESSION

Remember when I said that this journal was like boot camp? Well, consider yourself graduated. Congratulations! The following pages don't have any prompts or interruptions—they are reserved for you to free-write and practice everything you learned from the first parts of the journal. If you get stuck, turn back to this page and look at the list of questions from my therapist, Lori, for some inspiration.

Therapy has become such an important part of my life. It is another tool that helps me to understand, love, and forgive myself. It teaches me how to communicate honestly with others and, more important, with myself. I have been seeing my therapist since the summer of 2020. I meet with her once a week, and it's so cool to have someone who is so focused on my growth and encouraging me every step of the way.

Lori challenges me to evaluate the patterns in my life that aren't productive and create healthy boundaries. She has really helped me to release the internalized shame that I've developed from different life experiences. Our relationship has become very personal and very constructive. I've had breakthrough moments in therapy, when I was really able to scrutinize past mistakes while focusing on present actions, connecting the dots on why I responded and continue to respond in certain ways. When I do that, I can move forward and remain aware of my triggers so that I can learn to react in a way that serves me. A lot of that self-analysis comes from challenging questions. I wanted to share with you some of the questions that have helped me dive deep into who I am, who I was, and who I want to be. Here is a list of questions from my therapist, for you, so that, hopefully, you can experience the same kind of personal breakthroughs.

Lori encouraged me to change the way I journal and I want to challenge you to do the same: Record things beyond the simple events of each day. Dig beyond the facts and below the surface. Ask yourself: What emotion or mood did that event trigger? Write about how things made you feel and figure out why it made you feel that way. Document your emotional journey. Good luck, and God bless all the messy moments ahead!

Questions from Lori:
- How would people who love me describe me?
- What is one question I would like to answer this week?
- What is one change I can make in the next month that will make the biggest impact on me?
- I want more of . . . Why?
- I want less of . . . Why?
- What do I want to say yes to?
- What do I want to say no to?
- What do I get excited about?
- What do I really love about myself? List ten things.
- Choose an inspiration word for the week. What does it mean to you? And how can you live your life this week with that word in mind?
- Make a schedule for your perfect day. Take one of these things and do it sometime this week.
- If you couldn't fail, what would you do?
- What lesson did you learn the hard way?
- What can you do today that you couldn't do last year?
- What does your JOY look like today?
- If you had to teach something, what would you teach?
- Are you holding on to something you need to let go of?
- How do I find God in the midst of my *mess* right now?
- What is God teaching me in this moment? What are you going to do about it?

PART 2
FREEWRITING

Time to fly solo,
let loose!

Start date of your journaling journey →

"Owning our story and loving ourselves through that process is the bravest thing we will ever do."

—BRENÉ BROWN

Be strong and courageous, because you will lead these people to inherit the land I swore to their ancestors to give them. (JOSHUA 1:6)

Trust in the Lord with all your heart and
lean not on your own understanding. (PROVERBS 3:5)

_____

_____

_____

_____

_____

_____

_____

_____

_____

_____

_____

_____

_____

_____

_____

_____

_____

_____

_____

_____

_____

_____

"You can, you should, and if you're brave enough to start, you will."

—STEPHEN KING

Not only so, but we also glory in our sufferings, because
we know that suffering produces perseverance; perseverance,
character; and character, hope. (ROMANS 5:3-4)

Finally, brothers and sisters, whatever is true, whatever is noble, whatever is right, whatever is pure, whatever is lovely, whatever is admirable—if anything is excellent or praiseworthy— think about such things. (PHILIPPIANS 4:8)

"Instead of that anxiety about chasing a passion that you're not even feeling, do something that's a lot simpler: just follow your curiosity."

—ELIZABETH GILBERT

I praise you because I am fearfully and wonderfully made; your works are wonderful, I know that full well. (PSALMS 139:14)

Do not be anxious about anything, but in every situation, by prayer and petition, with thanksgiving, present your requests to God. (PHILIPPIANS 4:6)

"The difference between ordinary and extraordinary is that little extra."
—JIMMY JOHNSON

Search me, God, and know my heart; test me
and know my anxious thoughts. (PSALMS 139:23)

Do not conform to the pattern of this world, but be transformed by the renewing of your mind. Then you will be able to test and approve what God's will is—his good, pleasing and perfect will. (ROMANS 12:2)

"Well-behaved women seldom make history."
—LAUREL THATCHER ULRICH

So we fix our eyes not on what is seen, but on
what is unseen, since what is seen is temporary, but
what is unseen is eternal. (2 CORINTHIANS 4:18)

"The cure for anything is salt water: sweat, tears, or the sea."

—ISAK DINESEN

Above all, love each other deeply, because love
covers over a multitude of sins. (1 PETER 4:8)

"Speak your mind—even if your voice shakes."

—MAGGIE KUHN

May the God of hope fill you with all joy and peace
as you trust in him, so that you may overflow with hope
by the power of the Holy Spirit. (ROMANS 15:13)

_____

_____

_____

_____

_____

_____

_____

_____

_____

_____

_____

_____

_____

_____

_____

_____

_____

_____

_____

_____

_____

_____

"If we have our own why of life, we shall get along with almost any how."

—FRIEDRICH NIETZSCHE

Gracious words are a honeycomb, sweet to the soul
and healing to the bones. (PROVERBS 16:24)

"Perhaps our eyes need to be washed by our tears once in a while, so that we can see life with a clearer view again."

—ALEX TAN

In their hearts humans plan their course,
but the Lord establishes their steps. (PROVERBS 16:9)

"Be a fountain, not a drain."

—REX HUDLER

Let the king be enthralled by your beauty;
honor him, for he is your lord. (PSALMS 45:11)

"Storms make trees take deeper roots."

—DOLLY PARTON

She speaks with wisdom, and faithful instruction is on her tongue. She watches over the affairs of her household and does not eat the bread of idleness. (PROVERBS 31:26-27)

Woohoo! Congrats. You did it. You filled all the pages.
I hope you continue your journaling practice.

I highlighted the whole page, that's how grateful I am to these people.

ACKNOWLEDGMENTS

LISA SHARKEY—down to the tiniest flower on the page, you made sure I had everything the exact way I envisioned this journal to be. Thank you for always advocating for me and making sure this project turned out to be beautiful and inspiring.

MADDIE PILLARI—wow! You went above and beyond in every way to make sure this journal came to life. Your hardworking and dedication is unmatched, and I'm so thankful to have had you through this process. Without you, this wouldn't have been possible! Thank you times a billion!!!!

LORI OBERACKER—thank you for guiding me through the power of journaling on paper to create real changes in my life. The journal exercises you've given me have helped me in so many moments, and I'm so thankful you have allowed me to share with so many others. I am forever grateful for you!

MINDY UTAY—thank you for extending your knowledge and expertise to add even more amazing, life-changing content to this journal! I am so appreciative.

Thanks to MARTA SCHOOLER, LYNNE YEAMANS, AMANDA HONG, and everyone else on the HARPER DESIGN TEAM.

Thank you to STEPHANIE STISLOW for designing this book so beautifully.

Thank you to MAX STUBBLEFIELD, ALBERT LEE, JAMIE YOUNGENTOB, and the rest of my UTA TEAM.

Thank you to CLARE ANNE DARRAGH, STEPHANIE DAVIDSON, SHANE HEGEMAN, and the rest of my FRANK FAMILY for working so hard.

Thank you to ADAM KALLER, MELISSA FOX, and all the people at HJTH.

RESOURCES

If you want to find more information about how to improve your mental health, here is a collection of organizations, resources, and apps that can provide or help locate support.

Finding a Therapist

Psychology Today
psychologytoday.com is an excellent resource for finding a therapist near you. Therapists are listed by geographical areas with a profile of each therapist that highlights their areas of practice. Arrangements are made between you and the therapist.

My Wellbeing
mywellbeing.com is a site that matches you with a therapist who is a compatible based on a questionnaire you fill out and submit. You are given several therapists to interview based on certain criteria.

Alma
helloalma.com is a platform for finding a therapist to meet in person or online.

Talkspace
talkspace.com is a platform that virtually connects you to a licensed therapist. Rates are set by the site and sessions are online.

Betterhelp
betterhelp.com is a resource for online therapy. The website matches you with a therapist from their large network and sessions are online.

Verywell Mind
verywellmind.com is an award-winning resource for reliable, compassionate, and up-to-date information about mental health. The website has articles to help you find a therapist, figure out what therapy is best for you, and other information on how to get help and support.

Self-Care Apps

Calm
calm.com is a popular app for mindfulness, meditation, sleep, relaxation, and other coping skills for stress and anxiety. It is free with an option for membership.

Glo Yoga
glo.com offers livestream yoga, meditation, and Pilates classes with expert teachers from around the world.

Dharma
dharma.org offers online meditation, courses, and teachings from the Insight Meditation Society

Ten Percent Happier App
tenpercent.com offers a meditation app from #1 *New York Times* bestselling author Dan Harris. The app offers meditation practice and teachings for people new to meditation as well as seasoned practitioners.

Insight Timer
This is a meditation app with a very large free library of guided meditations for relaxation and sleep. The app is good for beginners getting started on a mindfulness practice.

Breathwrk
Breathwrk is an app that offers guided breathing exercises to calm your mind and reduce stress.

Moodfit
getmoodfit.com is a good overall mental health app for wellness and emotional health. The app includes features such as journaling, meditation, breathing, and other wellness tips in an interactive format.

Experts Who Helped with This Journal

Lori Oberacker, MS, LMHC
Licensed Mental Health Counselor
Professional/Personal Life Coach
goodgroundcounseling.com

Mindy Utay, LCSW, JD
Psychotherapy-Breathwork-Coaching
mindyutay.com